Discover

LIZ WATERS

TEST BOOK 1

Longman

Longman Group UK Ltd
Longman House, Burnt Mill, Harlow,
Essex CM20 2JE, England
and Associated Companies throughout the world.

First published 1988
Fifth impression 1990

Produced by Longman Singapore (Pte) Ltd.

Printed in Singapore

ISBN 0 582 03177-X

Test 1 (Lessons 1-5)

1 Write the numbers.

1 .one. . . . .

2 . . . .

3 . . . .

4 . . . .

5 . . . .

6 . . . .

7 . . . .

8 . . . .

9 . . . .

10 . . . .

Score: 9

2 Write in the bubbles.

Kate   John   Sue   Lucy   Miss Harris

I'm Andy.

1   2   3   4   5

Score: 5

3 Write the words in the correct sentences.

friend teacher mother brother sister father dog

Lucy is Kate's .sister. . . . .

1 Mrs Morgan is Kate's . . . .

2 Andy is Kate's . . . .

3 Mr Morgan is Kate's . . . .

4 Sue is Kate's . . . .

5 Miss Harris is Kate's . . . .

6 Mr Green is Andy's . . . .

7 John is Andy's . . . .

8 Big Ben is Kate's . . . .

Score: 8

4 Complete the conversation.

JOHN:	Hello.
SUE:	Hello. . . . .
JOHN:	How are you?
SUE:	(1) . . . .
JOHN:	This is my cat.
SUE:	(2) . . . .?
JOHN:	Her name's Diana. And this is my dog.
SUE:	(3) . . . .?
JOHN:	His name's Tarzan.
JOHN'S MUM:	John! John!
SUE:	(4) . . . .?
JOHN:	That's my mum.
SUE:	Good afternoon, Mrs Dawson.
JOHN'S MUM:	(5) . . . .
JOHN:	I must go. Goodbye.
SUE:	(6) . . . .

Score:
12

5 Complete the passage with the correct form of the verb *to be*.

This . *is* . . Andy's family. Mr and Mrs Morgan (1). . . . Andy's father and mother. Kate

(2). . . . . Andy's sister. Kate and Andy (3). . . . . twins. Lucy (4). . . . . Andy's little sister.

Cleopatra (5). . . . . the family's cat. Big Ben (6). . . . . the family's dog.

Score:
6

6 Write about your family.

. . . .

. . . .

Score:
10

. . . .

Score:
50

Test 2 (Lessons 6-10)

1 Write questions and answers about ages.

Bob (15) .How. old. are. you,. Bob.?....

.........I'm fifteen..............

1 Harry (13) ....

....

2 Sarah (10) ....

....

3 Kate (11) ....

....

4 John (12) ....

....

5 Miss Harris (26) ....

....

6 Mr Green (32) ....

....

7 Mr Morgan (40) ....

....

Score:
7

2 Complete the conversation by writing the girl's questions.

GIRL: .What's. your. name.?...........

JOHN: John Dawson

GIRL: (1) ....

JOHN: I'm twelve.

GIRL: (2) ....

JOHN: 32, Castle Street, Dover.

GIRL: (3) ....

JOHN: Dover 66221.

GIRL: (4) ....

JOHN: My favourite number's seven.

GIRL: (5) ....

JOHN: It's my calculator.

GIRL: (6) ....

JOHN: That's my dad. I must go. Bye!

Score:
12

3 Complete the crossword.

ACROSS   DOWN

1   1

4   2

5   3

6

|¹C|O|M|²P|U|T|E|³R|

4

5

6

Score:
6

3

4 Complete the conversation with Kate, using *Yes* or *No*.

SARAH: Hello, are you Kate Morgan?

KATE: .Yes, I am.................

SARAH: Are you Andy's sister?

KATE: (1) ....

SARAH: Are you twelve?

KATE: (2) .... I'm eleven.

SARAH: Is your school Castle Hill School?

KATE: (3) ....

SARAH: And is your address 43, Stratton Street?

KATE: (4) .... It's 65, Cliff Road.

SARAH: Is this your comic?

KATE: (5) .... It's Sue's comic.

Score: 10

5 Read the passage and circle the correct answer.

Andy has pictures of an elephant, a lion and a tiger in his book. The elephant has big ears. It's from Africa. It's nearly fifteen years old. It's a wild animal. The lion is a wild animal from Africa too. It's twelve years old. The tiger isn't from Africa. It's Indian. Andy also has a picture of a panda in his book. The panda is a wild animal from China but it is in a zoo in England now.

The elephant is (a) Indian.
                 (b) African.
                 (c) English.

1 It's (a) 5 years old.
        (b) 50 years old.
        (c) 15 years old.

2 The lion is (a) American.
               (b) Indian.
               (c) African.

3 It is (a) 2 years old.
         (b) 12 years old.
         (c) 20 years old.

4 The tiger is from (a) America.
                     (b) China.
                     (c) India.

5 The panda is (a) an American pet.
                (b) a Chinese wild animal.
                (c) a Chinese pet.

Score: 5

6 Write about an animal.

....

....

....

....

....

Score: 10

Score: 50

Test 3 (Lessons 11-15)

1 Write questions and answers.

Nikos/Greece (age 8)

.Who's. that. boy.?.................

.That's .Nikos.....................

.Where's. he. from.?.................

.He's. from .Greece.................

1 Severiano/Spain (age 42)

....

....

....

....

2 John/Britain (age 12)

....

....

....

....

3 Leila/Turkey (age 12)

....

....

....

....

4 Isabelle/France (age 30)

....

....

....

....

5 Eddie/USA (age 28)

....

....

....

....

Score:
10

2 Write the names of the objects with *a, an* or *some*.

. a .sweet..........

1 ....

2 ....

3 ....

4 ....

5 ....

6 ....

Score:
6

5

3 Write questions and answers about nationality.

Alan (USA)

.Are you American.? . . . .

.Yes, I am. . . . .

1 Sophia and Marta (Italy)

. . . .

. . . .

2 Franz and Heidi (Germany)

. . . .

. . . .

3 Ali and Husnu (Turkey)

. . . .

. . . .

4 Carlos (Argentina)

. . . .

. . . .

5 Yukiko (Japan)

. . . .

. . . .

6 Lena (Greece)

. . . .

. . . .

Score:
12

4 Complete the word puzzle.

1 The sky is . . . .

2 Kate's hair is . . . .

3 Grass is . . . .

4 An orange is . . . .

5 The sun is . . . .

6 A cloud is . . . .

7 A tomato is . . . .

Score:
6

5 Read the passage and answer the questions.

Will is from Chicago in the USA. He is a singer in the band
Shades. He is eighteen years old and he is good-looking. His
hair is blond and his eyes are blue. His favourite colour is red.

What nationality is Will?

He's American. . . . .

1 Where's he from in the USA?

. . . .

2 Is he a singer?

. . . .

3 How old is he?

. . . .

4 What colour is his hair?

. . . .

5 What colour are his eyes?

. . . .

6 What's his favourite colour?

. . . .

Score: 6

6 Now write about your favourite singer or a friend in the same way.

. . . .

. . . .

. . . .

. . . .

. . . .

. . . .

. . . .

. . . .

. . . .

. . . .

Score: 10

. . . .

Score: 50

. . . .

Test 4 (Lessons 16-20)

1 Write questions and answers about the clothes.

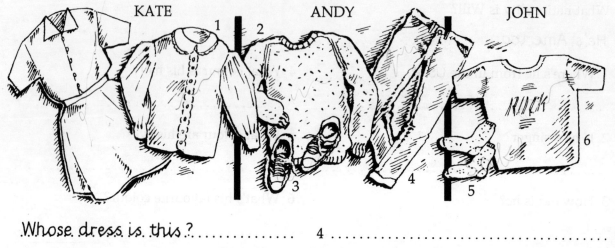

KATE   ANDY   JOHN

Whose dress is this? ....   4 ....

It's Kate's. ....

1 ....   5 ....

....

2 ....   6 ....

....

3 ....

....

2 Answer the questions, using *No* and *mine*.

Is this Kate's coat?

No, it isn't hers. It's mine. ....

1 Is this John's anorak?

....

2 Are these Andy's shoes?

....

3 Is this Mrs Morgan's skirt?

....

4 Are these Sue's boots?

....

5 Is this Miss Harris's book?

....

3 Find the words in the word snake.

BORINGGREATGOODHORRIBLEFANTASTIC

.boring. . . . .   3 . . . .

1 . . . .   4 . . . .

2 . . . .

Score:

4

4 Complete the conversation.

TINA: Hello, Bob.

BOB: Hi, Tina.

TINA: Look at my stamp collection.. .Have you got any. . foreign stamps?

BOB: Yes, I have.

TINA: (1) . . . .?

BOB: Nearly four hundred.

TINA: (2) . . . . .foreign coins?

BOB: No, I haven't, but my brother has.

TINA: (3) . . . .?

BOB: I think he's got nearly eighty.

TINA: (4) . . . . .German coins?

BOB: No, he hasn't.

TINA: This is my David Bowie badge. I think David Bowie's fantastic.

        (5) . . . . favourite pop star?

BOB: My favourite pop star? I don't know. I don't like pop music much.

TINA: You are funny!

Score:

10

5 Write the words in the correct column.

.....I..... .....my..... .....mine.

....

....

....

6 Read the information about Sue and write a paragraph about her.

Name:	Sue Wilson
Occupation:	Schoolgirl
Age:	12
Nationality:	British
Colour of hair:	Brown
Colour of eyes:	Brown
Favourite pop star:	Bob Marley
Collections:	Posters, pop star photos, stickers

Begin: ..Her name is Sue Wilson. She.......................

....

....

....

....

....

....

Test 5 (Lessons 21-25)

1 Read the passage, look at the picture and write the names of the rooms.

Our house has got seven rooms. Downstairs on the ground floor there is a sitting room, a dining room and a kitchen. Upstairs on the next floor there are two bedrooms and a bathroom. There's an attic in the roof. I think my bedroom is the best room in the house.

1 . dining room. . . . .

2 . . . .

3 . . . .

4 . . . .

5 . . . .

6 . . . .

7 . . . .

Score:
6

2 Now write questions and answers about the house.

bedroom/ground floor

.Is. there. a. bedroom. on. the. ground floor?

.No,. there. isn't. . . . .

1 kitchen/ground floor

. . . .

. . . .

2 bedroom/next floor

. . . .

. . . .

3 bathroom/ground floor

. . . .

. . . .

4 sitting room/upstairs

. . . .

. . . .

5 dining room/ground floor

. . . .

. . . .

6 attic/roof

. . . .

. . . .

Score:
12

11

3 Look at the picture and write questions or answers.

.Where's. the .table ? . . . .

It's next to the bed.

1 . . . .

It's on the wall.

2 . . . .

They're on the table.

3 . . . .

It's next to the door.

4 . . . .

It's under the bed.

5 Where's the chair?

. . . .

6 Where are the clothes?

. . . .

7 Where are the boots?

. . . .

8 Where are the toys?

. . . .

Score:

8

12

4 Write the points of the compass.

7_____→

6_____→

5_____→

4_____→

north _____

1_____

2_____

3_____

5 Read the passage and answer True (T) or False (F).

Cardiff is a large city on the south coast of Wales. It is the capital of Wales and a busy port. Boats go in and out of Cardiff every day. There are lots of interesting things to see in Cardiff. There's a museum and a beautiful university and in the centre of the city there's an old castle.

Cardiff is in Wales. ..T...

1 It is in the centre of Wales. .....

2 It is big. .....

3 It is busy. .....

4 There aren't any boats in Cardiff. .....

5 There are many interesting things to see. .....

6 The museum is boring. .....

7 The castle is in the centre of the university. .....

6 Write about a town or city in your country.

. . . .

. . . .

. . . .

. . . .

. . . .

. . . .

. . . .

. . . .

Test 6 (Lessons 26-30)

1 Write questions and answers.

radio/calculator

Do you want a radio or a calculator for your birthday?

Can I have a radio, please?

1 cassette/record

....

....

2 brush/wallet

....

....

3 sweets/chocolates

....

....

4 trousers/shoes

....

....

5 coat/jacket

....

....

6 stickers/posters

....

....

Score:
12

2 Write the words.

CHORT *torch* 1 MERAAC .... 2 CHAWT ....

3 RODERC .... 4 SERUP .... 5 LAWELT ....

Score:
5

14

3 Complete the crossword.

1 She's . . . . . the guitar.

2 She's . . . . . to the radio.

3 She's . . . . . her homework.

4 He's . . . . . TV.

5 He's . . . . . a book.

6 She's . . . . . a letter.

4 Look at the pictures and write questions and answers about the people.

Sarah/watch/TV

Is Sarah watching TV.? . . . .

No, she isn't. . . . .

1 Tina/read/book

. . . .

. . . .

2 Jack/read/book

. . . .

. . . .

3 Mary/do/homework

. . . .

. . . .

4 Robert/listen/radio

. . . .

. . . .

5 Ann/play/guitar

. . . .

. . . .

5 Look at the questionnaire about Robert and write questions and answers.

	Yes	No
speak Spanish?		✗
1 ride a bicycle?	✓	
2 use a computer	✓	
3 climb a rope?		✗
4 play the guitar?	✓	
5 make chocolates?		✗
6 use a calculator?	✓	

. Can you speak Spanish?............

. No, I can't......................

1 ....
....

2 ....
....

3 ....
....

4 ....
....

5 ....
....

6 ....
....

Score: 12

6 Look at the picture and write about what the people are doing.

....
....
....
....
....
....
....
....
....
....
....

Score: 10

Score: 50

16

Test 7 (Lessons 31-35)

1 Write the words in the correct boxes.

milkshake
salt
pepper
tomato soup
milk
tea
apple pie
hamburger
mustard
onions
chicken
coffee
chips
tomato ketchup
fish and chips

FOOD	THINGS TO GO WITH FOOD	DRINKS
		milkshake

Score: 7

2 Complete the conversation in a fish and chip shop.

MAN: Next, please.

MR BROWN: *What do you want* . . . ., Tina?

TINA: (1) . . . . fish and chips, please?

MR BROWN: Two fish and chips, please.

MAN: (2) . . . . salt?

TINA: No, thank you.

MAN: (3) . . . . tomato ketchup?

TINA: No, thank you. (4) . . . . tomato ketchup.

Oh, (5) . . . . a Coca-Cola, please, Dad?

MR BROWN: OK. Two Coca-Colas, please.

Score: 10

3 Write the sentences using *one* or *ones*.

I/blue trainers/ green ones

.I. like .the .blue. trainers. but .I .don't. like. the. green ones...................

1 Kate/black skirt/pink skirt

....

2 John/red sports bag/blue sports bag

....

3 Sue/black anorak/white anorak

....

4 I/pink roller skates/silver roller skates

....

5 Andy/grey shorts/yellow shorts

....

Score:
5

4 Write questions and answers about the subjects.

Do. you. like. Science.?

Yes,. I. do...........

So. do. I..........

3 ....
✓ ....
....

1 ....
✓ ....
....

4 ....
✗ ....
....

2 ....
✗ ....
....

5 ....
✗ ....
....

Score:
10

18

5 Find the activities and write them.

I like...

WINDSURFINGWATERSKIINGDOINGGYMNASTICSVISITINGMUSEUMSCLIMBING
PAINTINGCANOEINGPLAYINGFOOTBALLBIRDWATCHING

windsurfing ....

1 ....   5 ....

2 ....   6 ....

3 ....   7 ....

4 ....   8 ....

Score:
8

6 Write a letter to a penfriend. Write about your family, your school and your favourite sports and activities.

....

....

....

....

....

....

....

....

....

....

Score:
10

Score:
50

....

Test 8 (Lessons 36-40)

1 Answer the questions about the animals. Choose from the animals below.

anteater   giraffe   leopard   zebra   crab   monkey   elephant

Which animal has got a long neck?   .A.giraffe. . . . .

1 Which animal has got black and white stripes? . . . .

2 Which animal has got long arms?   . . . .

3 Which animal has got big spots?   . . . .

4 Which animal has got a hard shell?   . . . .

5 Which animal has got big ears?   . . . .

6 Which animal has got a long tongue?   . . . .

Score:

6

2 Complete the crossword. Write the opposites.

DOWN
1 ugly
2 small
3 dirty
5 soft
6 fat

ACROSS
4 cheap
5 cold
7 slow

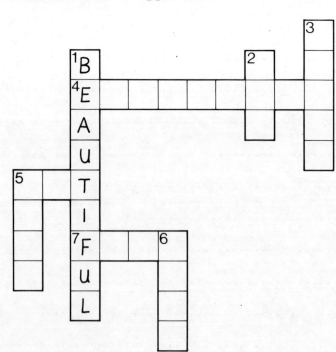

Score:

7

20

3 Write the words.

mm .millimetre.....................

1 cm .... 4 in ....

2 m .... 5 ft ....

3 km .... 6 yd ....

4 Write questions and answers.

.How.tall.is.he.?..................... 1m 35cm

He's.one.metre,.thirty-five.centimetres.tall.

1 .... 2.5m

....

2 .... 3000m

....

3 .... 2m

....

4 .... 1m

....

5 .... 250km   London → Manchester

....

5 Complete the sentences.

(quiet) You are speaking too .quietly. . . . .

1 (quick) He is walking too . . . .

2 (slow) She is running very . . . .

3 (cold) The sea is very . . . .

4 (loud) The TV is too . . . .

5 (loud) They are singing . . . .

6 (quiet) You are whispering too . . . .

7 (difficult) This question is very . . . .

8 (quick) They are talking too . . . .

Score:

8

6 Read the passage and answer True (T) or False (F).

The Amazon River is in South America. It's very long: nearly
6,450km long, and very wide. Near the sea it's 240km wide. The
river starts in the Andes Mountains in the west, goes through the
Amazon jungle, where there are lots of very tall trees, and finally
goes to the sea. There are lots of animals in the jungle and lots of
fish in the river. There aren't many people in the jungle. It's hot
and wet but I like it because it's beautiful.

The Amazon River is in Europe. . .F. .

1 It isn't very long. . . . . .

2 It's very wide. . . . . .

3 There are many trees in the jungle. . . . . . .

4 The river starts in the jungle. . . . . .

5 It goes to the sea. . . . . .

6 There are many fish in the river. . . . . .

7 There aren't many animals in the jungle. . . .

8 It's cold. . . . . .

Score:

8

7 Write about a river, a mountain or a building.

. . . .

. . . .

. . . .

. . . .

. . . .

. . . .

. . . .

Score:

10

. . . .

Score:

50

Test 9 (Lessons 41-45)

1 Write the prices.

5p   .five pence........

1 £1   ....

2 £1.50   ....

3 £2.50   ....

4 £5   ....

5 £9.60   ....

Score: 5

2 Write questions and answers about the price of food.

.How much are the peaches ?........

.They're twenty pence each........

1 ....

....

2 ....

....

3 ....

....

4 ....

....

5 ....

....

Score: 10

23

3 Write the time.

It's four o'clock. .... 3 ....

1 .... 4 ....

2 .... 5 ....

4 Complete the word puzzle with weather words.

What's the weather like?

It's ...

```
              ¹W
    ²F  ³R    E  ☐  ☐  ☐  ☐
        ☐     T
    ⁴S  ☐  ☐  ☐
    ⁵S  ☐  ☐  ☐  ☐  G
        ☐
```

5 Look at Jack and Tina's morning routines. Write the questions and answers.

7.30   get up
7.35   have a shower
7.50   get dressed
8.00   have breakfast
8.15   go to school

What time do they get up? .... 3 ....

They get up at half past seven. ....

1 .... 4 ....

  ....

2 ....

  ....

24

6 Now look at Sue's evening routine and write questions and answers.

4.30	get home from school
4.50	have tea
5.45	do homework
7.00	watch television
9.20	go to bed

.What. time .does .she. get .home .from .school .? . . . .

.She .gets .home .at .half .past .four. . . . .

1 . . . .

. . . .

2 . . . .

. . . .

3 . . . .

. . . .

4 . . . .

. . . .

Score:	
	8

7 Write a letter to a friend about your daily routine.

. . . .

. . . .

. . . .

. . . .

. . . .

. . . .

. . . .

. . . .

Score:	
	10

Score:	
	50

. . . .

Test 10 (Lessons 46-50)

1 Write the phrases in the correct column.

Monday   6 o'clock
the autumn   Saturday
3rd April   4th October
May   the evening
Saturday evening   the winter
the morning

IN the autumn	ON	AT

Score: 10

2 Write about what people like or don't like.

chocolate   fish soup   mice

...He likes chocolate....   1 ....   2 ....

icecream   mice   ballet

3 ....   4 ....   5 ....

Score: 5

3 Complete the dialogue.

SUE: When's Alan's birthday?

KATE: ...... It's on .... 1st January.

SUE: (1) .... buy him a present.

KATE: OK. What (2) .... buy him?

SUE: (3) .... he like chocolates?

KATE: No, (4) .... But he (5) .... games.

     (6) .... get him a computer game.

SUE: (7) ....?

KATE: Oh! They're £7. (8) .... too expensive.

     (9) .... a jigsaw.

SUE: OK. They're only £4.

Score: 9

4 Write sentences.

Kate	Sue	Andy
often	often	never

...Kate and Sue often do the washing up...

...Andy never does the washing up...

1

Kate	Sue	Andy
never	sometimes	never

. . . .

. . . .

2

Kate	Sue	Andy
sometimes	never	sometimes

. . . .

. . . .

3

Kate	Sue	Andy
usually	never	never

. . . .

. . . .

Score:

6

27

5 Complete the questions and answers.

..Does............John buy sweets?

Yes, he does.............

1 ....you help in the house?

Yes,....................

2 .... Kate get up early?

Yes,....................

3 .... John play video games?

No, ...

4 .... Kate and Andy live in London?

No,.....................

5 .... you do the washing up?

No,..................... .

Score:
5

6 Read the passage and circle the correct answer.

Simon Crawford is twenty years old. He is from Dover but at the moment he is living and studying in London. He's training to be a teacher and he's doing a four-year course at a college in the centre of the city.

"Teaching is hard work but I like it. My subjects are Maths and Computer Science and I think they're very interesting."

From Monday to Friday Simon studies every evening but on Saturday he goes to the cinema with his girlfriend. She is training to be a teacher too.

At the end of his course, Simon wants to find a teaching job in Dover.

Simon is from (a) Dover (b) London.

1 He's living in (a) Dover (b) London.
2 He's training to be (a) a teacher
  (b) a doctor.
3 He (a) likes (b) doesn't like Maths.
4 He goes to the cinema (a) every day
  (b) at the weekend.
5 At the end of his course he wants to live
  (a) in London (b) in Dover.

Score:
5

7 Now write about the life of an adult you know.

....

....

....

....

....

....

Score:
10

Score:
50

28